Storing
CARBON

Plants

Plants need carbon to grow.

Where is the carbon?

The carbon is in the leaves.

The carbon is in the stem.

The carbon is in the roots.

leaves

stem

roots

The carbon will

stay in the plants.

This will help to keep the world **clean.**

Forests have plants

Look at the trees.

The trees will

keep lots of carbon.

This will help to keep the world clean.

Grasslands have plants

Look at the grass.

The grass is long.

The grass will
keep lots of carbon.

This will help to
keep the world clean.

Farms have plants

This **farm** has sugar cane.

This farm has rice.

This farm has wheat.

The plants on the farms will keep lots of carbon.

14

This will help to

keep the world clean.

Glossary

clean

farm